D0178624

About the Author

Hi, I'm Choly Knight, and I'm a total geek for all kinds of cartoon and gaming culture! I'm constantly sewing and crafting cool things for myself and for friends inspired by TV shows like Pokémon and Adventure Time and games like Minecraft! It's one of my greatest pleasures to take the beautiful, creative ideas found in games and TV shows that I'm a fan of and find a way to make them physical and tangible. Sometimes you can buy fan items from games, shows, and books, but I love to challenge myself and craft things with my own two hands.

I have been crafting for as long as I can remember, and have drawn, painted, sculpted, and stitched everything in sight. After studying studio art and earning a BA in English, I now enjoy trying to find numerous different ways to combine my passions for writing, fine art, and craft art. I focus on handcrafted clothing, accessories, and other creations inspired by Japanese art, anime, and style, and I specialize in cosplay (costume play) hats and hoodies.

I've had fun writing many sewing books that feature my cool, whimsical designs, like *Sew Kawaii!*, *Sew Your Own Pet Pillows*, *Sew Baby*, *Sewing Stylish Handbags & Totes*, *Sew Me! Sewing Basics*, *Sew Me! Sewing Home Decor*, and *Sew Me! Sewing Accessories*. I also love using all sorts of mediums besides fabric to craft, and have published books about the fun stuff I've made with products like duct tape (*Awesome Duct Tape Projects*) and decoden (*Bling It Up!*). You can find out more about me and my work on my website: *www.cholyknight.com*.

Welcome to a Pixel World!

You've been living in a pixel world whether you've realized it or not. Pixel art is a rising trend in a number of fields and has been garnering quite a bit of positive attention in recent years. Video games, art, architecture, interior design, handicrafts, and more are all being influenced every day by what we see and engage with on the screens of our computers, TVs, and mobile devices. But even though nowadays resolutions have skyrocketed and animation has advanced by leaps and bounds, there are plenty of people who are calling back to the nostalgic, inspiring world of pixels.

Now, this book could have been much, much longer if we had attempted to cover more areas related to pixel art. There is a rich history behind it and plenty of applications for it in the modern day. But time, demand, and budgets prevailed, and we decided to focus on one game: the international gem Minecraft, which maps 2-D pixel art onto a 3-D world and thrives on the players' creativity and imagination.

There are other video games we could have included in this book, but none of them seemed so ideal for the artistic crafter as Minecraft, since aspects of and items from the game can be easily translated into both 2-D and 3-D real-life items. And unlike many other games, Minecraft is not only family-friendly, but also appeals to a wide range of ages. It is not just for little kids—plenty of creative adults have discovered how fun and fulfilling it is to create worlds rather than destroy enemies.

On the next few pages, you'll find just a taste of the various historical and artistic roots of what we are calling pixel art. Between these images of inspiration, the small-scale hands-on projects that are taught in this book, and the gallery of ways in which other fans have brought the game to life, we hope that your imagination and artistry are primed and that you are ready to challenge yourself to get creating.

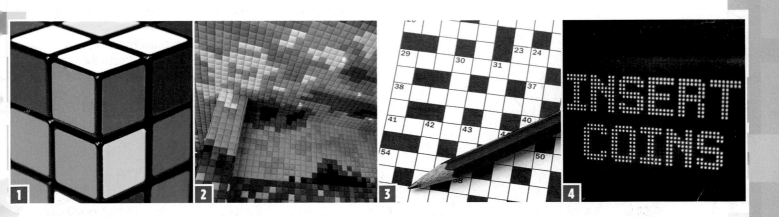

1 **Rubik's Cube®.** A popular toy using pixels, the Rubik's Cube®, was invented in 1974. The object of the brainteaser is to turn the puzzle in order to get all six sides of the cube a solid color.

2 **Pixel wall art in a restaurant in Brussels, Belgium.** 2-D pixels are easy to map onto flat surfaces such as walls, and plenty of modern interior design has taken its cue from the pixel plan in a way that was not seen in the past.

3 **Crossword puzzle.** Pixels are even found in word games like crossword puzzles. Just as the grid and the pixel lend themselves to easy and simple design, so do they allow for a logical and easy-to-follow word game.

4 **Classic pixel-based game screen.** Though you can see that the actual pixels themselves are rounded, this is a classic example of where pixels got their start: in gaming, constrained by the screens on which the games had to appear.

5 Cross stitch of a flower. Considered the oldest type of embroidery, cross stitching involves sewing Xs in a grid following a pattern, so designs are build with each X stitch as a kind of "pixel."

6 Ancient mosaic in Analipsi, Greece, dating from the 5th century AD. Mosaic tile art, used on walls, in baths, and more is one of the most recognizable forms of pixel-esque art. The main difference is that the individual "pixel" or pieces of the mosaic don't necessarily follow a square grid.

7 Peg arrangement for physical pixels. These pegs are rounded but together clearly form a pixel image.

8 Lite-Brite® pegs. Lite-Brite® is a toy created in 1967 that consisted of a light box with a grid of holes into which you place colored translucent pegs that glow. It was very popular with children and making designs on the grid was easy for anyone.

9 Mondrian-inspired interior design. Dutch painter Piet Mondrian's famous works, which feature intersecting lines creating square and rectangular shapes reminiscent of pixels, inspired this interior design.

10 Urban art in East Village, New York City. Pixel art can be painted, made from tiles, or made from blocks, which makes it a popular choice for street art.

11 Pixel Painter program. This pixel-based painting program is simple enough for a child, but a math-savvy adult can also link in equations to auto-generate designs. It makes pixel design accessible to anyone right at their fingertips. Download free at *demonstrations.wolfram.com/PixelPainter*.

12 Modern mosaic.

13 Kitchen tiles. Most people see pixels every single day—they are often found in bathroom or kitchen tiling or flooring.

14 Building blocks. Building blocks are like pixels in a 3-D world.

15 Patchwork quilt. Classic patchwork involves sewing together textile squares to create a whole design. Though patchwork also involves sewing together other shapes, the square is where it has its roots.

16 Legos®. One of the most well-known toys of the twentieth century is Legos®, interlocking building blocks that come in an array of colors and sizes but that are square and rectangular in design, resulting in creations very similar to pixelated art.

17 Bomb graffiti from a wall in Poland.

18 Pixel building in Poznań, Poland. Modern building design has moved away from the elaborate and toward simple, sometimes boxy and pixelated designs.

19 Crocheted patchwork blanket.

20 Game console street art featuring a Space Invader.

21 Mosaic in Turkey.

22 Cross stitch snowflake.

23 Sprite urban art made from tiles.

24 Pixel building. The Wanangkura Stadium in Australia is a fabulous example of pixel architecture, with pixels both inside and out.

25 Lite-Brite® pumpkin art.

26 Modern patchwork quilt.

27 Space Invaders alien. Space Invaders is an arcade game released 1978 that enjoyed immense popularity; the aliens featured in this pixel-based game have become iconic.

28 Landscaping squares. The tile and grass design of this modern landscaped patio follows a pixelated organizational scheme.

29 Cross stitch of owls.

5

10

15

20

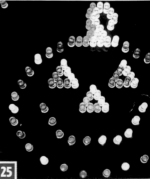

25

Talk to Me: Design and the Communication between People and Objects by Paola Antonelli. This book, based on a 2011 exhibit at the Museum of Modern Art, includes discussion of pixel projects. Excerpt from the book: "We now expect objects to communicate, a cultural shift made evident when we see children searching for buttons or sensors on a new object, even when the object has no batteries or plug. [This book] thrives on this important late-twentieth-century development in the culture of design, which can be described as a shift from the centrality of function to that of meaning, and on the twenty-first-century focus on the need to communicate in order to exist."

Talk to Me

Design and the Communication between People and Objects

MoMA

FRESH FROM THE OVEN

Cakes, cookies, cupcakes, and more make great game-inspired treats to enjoy! Many people have gotten creative with ingredients, food coloring, and designs to make personalized birthday cakes, party cakes, and just plain old tasty treats for any occasion. Get ready for a mouth-watering display of creativity!

Steve and friends cake by Angie Lee

Creeper rice krispy treats by Halle Harrington

A real game cake and grass brownies by Caroline "CazGirl" Richardson

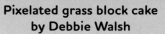
Pixelated grass block cake
by Debbie Walsh

Creeper and pig cupcakes
by Loren Ebert

Iced cookies by
Janine Eshelbrenner

Brownie, rice krispy treat, and
jello cake by Mellisa Swigart

PARTY TIME

Many parents have thrown game-inspired parties for their children, and adults like a good themed party too! Whether you're turning 10 or 100, anyone who loves the game will love these fun ideas for party favors, foods, setups, and more.

Grass party dining setup by Carol Colón (Partylicious)

Cheese lava party food by Melissa Smith

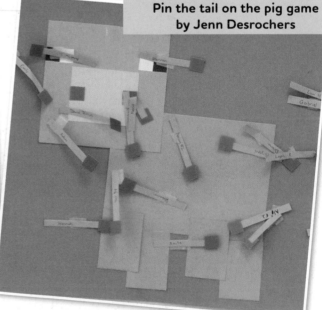

Pin the tail on the pig game by Jenn Desrochers

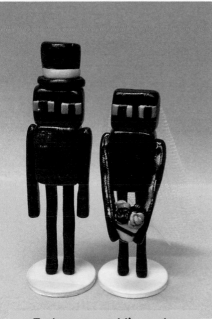

Creeper gift bags by Margarette Sia

Enderman wedding cake
toppers by Rin Smith

Licorice TNT
by Margarette Sia

Party setup by Margarette Sia

HOME SWEET HOME

Just like in the game, it feels good to come home to your very own room full of goodies and personalized decorations. Some fans have created entire Minecraft bedrooms and home goods inspired by the game for a real-life homey feeling.

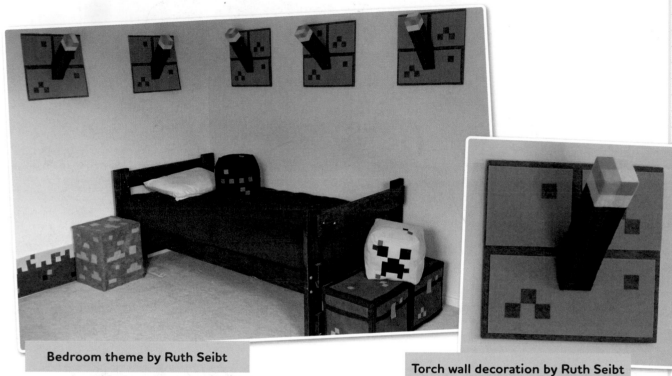

Bedroom theme by Ruth Seibt

Torch wall decoration by Ruth Seibt

Creeper lanterns by Laura Hutchison

Pillows by Gina House

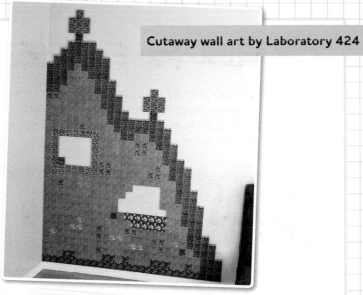

Cutaway wall art by Laboratory 424

Door plaque by Gem Battle

THAT'S A VERY NICE ROOM YOU HAVE THERE...

Bedroom theme by Gina House

CELEBRATE THE HOLIDAYS

Why not try a crossover from the game to a holiday? These people did! Whether you want a themed Christmas, Halloween, Valentine's Day, or your other favorite holiday, there are plenty of creative ways to make it happen. Get inspired by these ideas!

Crocheted Enderman ornament by Tina Stapleford

Clay Christmas wolf by Tina Vuotto

Cardboard box Christmas tree by Tyler Parkerson

Mosaic ornaments by Denise Bertacchi

Creeper pumpkin by ceemdee

TNT YOU'RE DYNAMITE

Valentine's Day bag toppers by L. Topp

Carved Creeper gourds and peppers by Brenda Ponnay

FANTASTIC FAN ART

The game has inspired countless artists to express themselves in amazing ways, from creating everything from comical drawings to dramatic illustrations. With as much fodder for the imagination as the game provides, it's no wonder that people are making remarkable works of art like the ones shown here!

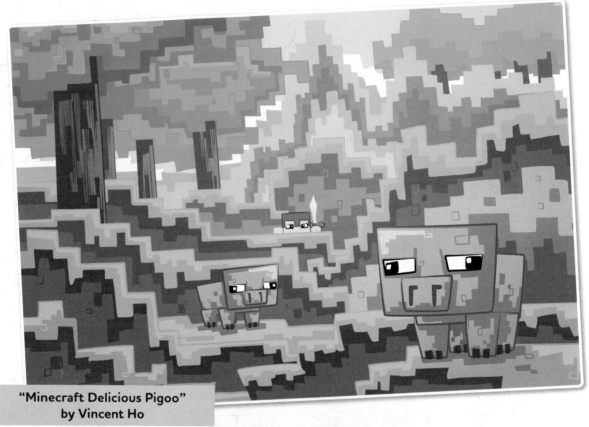

"Minecraft Delicious Pigoo"
by Vincent Ho

"Minecraft Plains Village"
by Declan Bachwirtz

"Ship and Lighthouse Minecraft
Render" by Declan Bachwirtz

Digital painting by
Tina Alfredsen

"A Night in Minecraft"
by Anna Allen

"Minecraft!" by William C. Jones

THE GAME

In case you're unfamiliar with how Minecraft works, here's a quick primer to give you an idea about the inspiration for all of the projects in this book.

THE PROTAGONIST

While the identity of the player is not an important aspect of the game, that doesn't stop fans from fawning over the simple pixelated human that you play as in the world of Minecraft. His name is Steve, and he's the person you control as you build, fight, and create your way through the game. Console versions of the game enable you to download different player skins so you can change how your character looks, but if you love classic Steve, you can bring him to life with the Cardboard Costume Head project (page 36).

THE CREATURES

The Minecraft world is filled with a strange but fun array of peaceful and hostile characters. Depending on what setting you play, you can encounter enemies (known as mobs) such as Creepers, Endermen, Zombies, Spiders, and more. They all behave differently and can net you special items when you defeat them. You'll also find friendly creatures like pigs, cows, and sheep, which have their own special attributes, too.

- **Creepers** are perhaps the most infamous Minecraft characters. These little green creatures love to silently sneak up on you in dark places, then explode with barely a warning, usually breaking away some of your hard work in the process.

- **Endermen** are dark and mysterious slender entities. They are teleporting creatures that show up and do little harm besides grabbing a random block or two. But look them in the eye and they start to attack!

- **Zombies** are classic enemies that show up at night, due to the fact that they catch fire in the daytime. They will frequently come after you in your home and try to break down your door if it's not strong enough.

- **Animals** range from chickens to pigs, cows, and even squid. The farmyard animals are harmless, and you can even breed and house them to create your own little farm for gathering eggs and milk.

To make your own crafted versions of these creatures, check out the Duct Tape Wallet (page 30), the Felt Plush Cube (page 50), and the Crocheted Creeper (page 52).

Shh, do you hear the hissing of a Creeper? It's so easy to feel like you're living the game when you accessorize with the cool Cardboard Costume Head (page 36) and a screen printed t-shirt (page 46)!

THE ENVIRONMENT

The amazing thing about Minecraft is the way in which you can use the environment around you to create whatever you can imagine. Stone can be mined and rebuilt into houses, sand can be collected and melted into glass, or diamonds can be mined and built into tools—you name it! As you explore the game, you're bound to find loads of different terrain and building materials, all of which act differently when you craft or build with them. Make your own versions of building materials with the Ore Light (page 40) or the Building Blocks (page 42).

THE CRAFTING

Where the real creativity starts to come into play is the craft part of Minecraft. You can combine raw materials collected from the world around you to create better building supplies, tools, food, potions, armor, farming equipment, and even electrically powered carts. You can find loads of tips and tricks on how to craft different items from the Internet, though you'll find that lots of happy accidents can occur by placing unusual items in the right pattern on your crafting table. Craft your own tools by checking out the Foam Tools project (page 32) or the Flashlight Torch (page 38).

Whatever you can create or imagine in the world of Minecraft is yours for the taking here. Just get a few simple supplies and you'll be making real-world versions of all your favorite Minecraft characters and game elements in no time!

Whether you tackle the tricky but awesome Crocheted Creeper project (page 52) or a simple Pixel Plant (page 26), you're going to love all the possibilities of things you can make with this book!

Understanding Project Difficulties

While all projects in this book are suitable for beginners, some are harder than others. Get an idea of what you're in for by following the chart here.

 Noob: These projects are practically foolproof! Ideal for complete beginners.

 Level+1: Simple and straightforward projects, but take just a bit more skill to get just right.

 Level+2: Has a technique or two that you might want to test out first, but otherwise simple.

 Level+3: Will take a bit longer, and you might have some trial-and-error moments.

 Level MAX: You might need some practice before trying these projects; they will take a few afternoons of work.

SUPPLIES

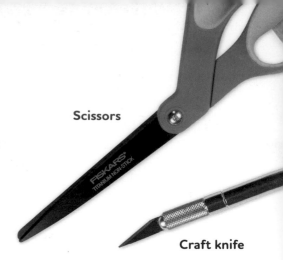

In this book you'll find projects that use a lot of different materials, from Perler beads to duct tape to paper. There are also a few basic tools that are good to have on hand no matter which projects you decide to tackle. And depending on the project you choose, you may need to get some additional crafting supplies. All of the supplies listed here are easy to find at your local craft store.

Scissors

Craft knife

THE BASICS

Ruler: Most of the projects in this book involve some kind of measuring, and a precise ruler will be a big help down the line. A sturdy metal ruler is great, though gridded transparent quilting rulers are a big help with measuring squares and rectangles.

Cutting mat: A self-healing cutting mat makes an ideal work surface. Not only does it absorb cuts from a craft knife, but it's also great for laying out duct tape pieces before they're joined to a project. A mat with a 1" (2.5cm) grid works double duty for measuring as well.

Craft knife/scissors: For perfectly straight cuts, a craft knife works wonders in conjunction with a ruler. Be sure to use it with care, because the blade is extremely sharp. A pair of reliable craft scissors will also do the job and are also great for reaching hard-to-cut areas. If you're working with duct tape, non-stick scissors are a real bonus.

Glue: The proper adhesives will make a world of difference for the paper crafting and Perler bead projects in this book. To keep things simple, hot glue works for most purposes, while rubber cement is ideal for paper crafting.

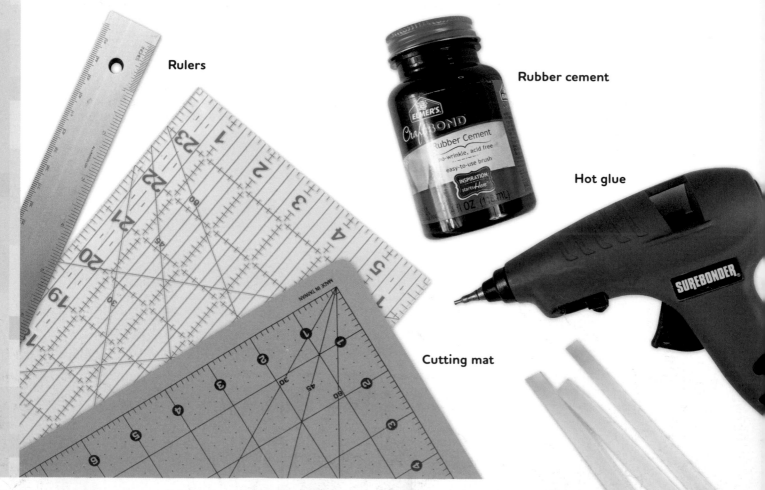

Rulers

Rubber cement

Hot glue

Cutting mat

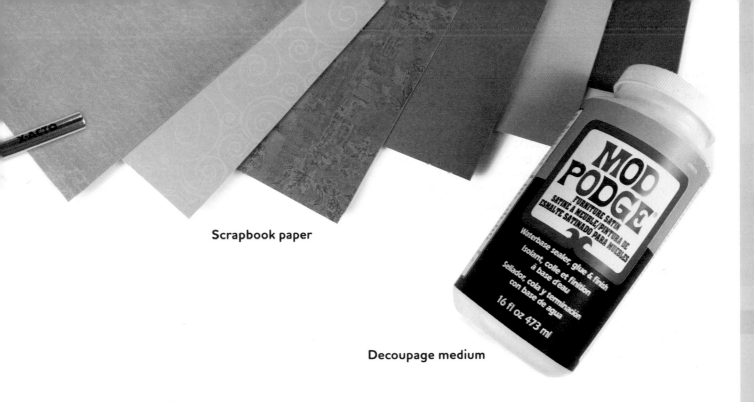

Scrapbook paper

Decoupage medium

FOR PAPER CRAFTING

Scrapbook paper: Colorful and plentiful, scrapbook paper is perfect for assembling the pixel patterns found in Minecraft, as it's sturdy enough to handle lots of gluing and folding. Use solid colors if you're a pixel purist, or try out patterned paper to give projects some depth and texture.

Decoupage medium: After meticulously working on paper craft pixel projects, you can use a decoupage medium like Mod Podge to give them extra shelf life. A few coats of this finish will seal up the paper so the edges are less likely to peel over time.

FOR FABRIC CRAFTS

Fleece: For beginners and kids, nothing beats fleece for ease and versatility! Fleece is very soft and simple to work with because the edges don't fray like most fabrics. You'll find it also comes in loads of fantastic colors, making it perfect for crafting the spectrum of objects in Minecraft.

Felt: Ideal for small crafts, felt is another fabulous fabric that is easy and reliable. Acrylic and wool varieties both work well, though felt blends with higher wool content tend to behave more predictably.

Fleece

Felt

FOR PERLER BEADS

Beads: Perler beads, also called Hama beads, are pixel-like plastic beads that fuse together when melted with an iron. The medium (5mm) size is most common, though mini (2.6mm) sizes can be found as well. Mini Perler beads are not as common in stores, so you might need to scour the Internet to find them and their corresponding boards. They fuse together beautifully for very small projects like jewelry.

Boards: Perler beads work in conjunction with plastic peg boards. These boards have a peg layout that allows you to set Perler beads in place (tweezers are a big help with this!) in a specified pattern. The boards come in different shapes and sizes, as well as in squares that can link up with others for really big creations.

Ironing supplies: To finish a Perler bead creation, it must be ironed so the beads melt just enough to fuse to each other. Most Perler bead kits come with an ironing paper, but parchment paper works just as well. A heavy and sturdy iron (with the steam turned off) is the ideal tool for fusing the beads.

PERLER BEAD QUICK START GUIDE

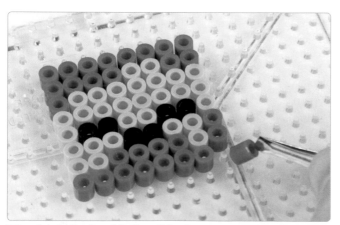

1 Create the bead design. Using tweezers, arrange the beads on the peg board following the chosen pattern, matching colors and placement. Working one row at a time or one color at a time often works the best for most people.

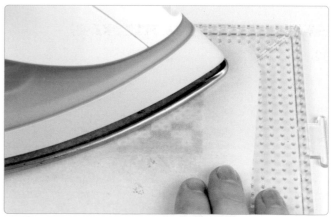

2 Iron each side. With the beaded board on a flat surface, place the ironing paper on top. Set an iron to medium heat and run it over the beads in circles until you can see the plastic melting and sticking to the paper. When finished, let the beads cool for a minute. Remove the piece from the board and iron the other side in the same way.

FOR DUCT TAPE

Tape: Durable, colorful, and easy to assemble, duct tape is a great material for beginning crafters. It comes in loads of different colors, finishes, and patterns, so you're bound to find one that matches the exact Minecraft item you're making. If you have the cutting supplies mentioned before—scissors, craft knife, ruler, and cutting mat—working with it will be much easier. Here are a few helpful techniques to keep in mind when creating the duct tape projects in this book.

MAKING DOUBLE-SIDED SHEETS

1 Create the back side. Layer strips of duct tape, sticky side down, on a cutting mat. Overlap them by about ¼" (0.5cm) to make a shape a little larger than the size of the sheet you need. When finished, trim the sheet to get the exact size you need.

2 Create the front side. Flip the sheet over (sticky side up) and layer it with more strips of duct tape as in step 1. Cover the sheet entirely, including about ½" (1.5cm) extending on all sides.

3 Finish the edges. Remove the sheet from the work surface and trim the corners at a diagonal. Fold over the sticky extensions to the back so all the edges are finished.

MAKING DUCT TAPE STICKERS

1 Trace the design. Use a pencil to trace the sticker design onto a sheet of parchment paper.

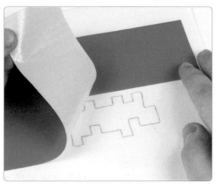

2 Apply the tape. Flip the paper over and apply tape over the design so it is completely covered.

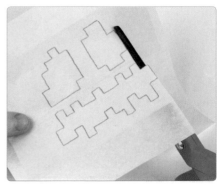

3 Cut out the design. Cut around the traced design to complete the sticker. When you're ready to use it, simply peel the parchment paper off the back of the tape sticker.

FOR CROCHET

Yarn: The Crocheted Creeper project (page 52) calls for a bit of crochet knowledge, so if you're new to the craft, here's a good way to break in. You'll find a large yarn selection at your local craft store. Beginners should use a yarn that is both large and smooth—nothing too fluffy or decorative. It's quite easy to find extremely soft and cozy yarns that fit that description; just be sure the yarn label states that it's "bulky" or "chunky" or creates 3.5-1.5 stitches per inch (sts/in).

Hooks: The yarn you choose will need an accompanying crochet hook that matches it in size. You'll want to get a hook that's a size or two smaller than the manufacturer recommends on the yarn label of your chosen yarn to create tighter stitches for the Crocheted Creeper.

Crochet basics: To get started with a project like the Crocheted Creeper, here are the basic crochet stitches you'll need to know. If it's your first time crocheting, you'll see it takes a bit of time to get used to handling the hook and yarn, but if you have a thick yarn and a large hook the process should feel natural pretty soon.

●● **GAMER TIP** ●●

THE ONE RULE

Never dig straight down. Eventually, you'll run into lava and lose everything you've collected along the way!

MAKING THE FOUNDATION CHAIN

1 Create the loop. The first step is to create a slip knot with the yarn. Begin by making a loop with one end of the yarn. The tail should be the bottom layer of the loop. The working yarn should lay on top and is the end attached to the yarn ball.

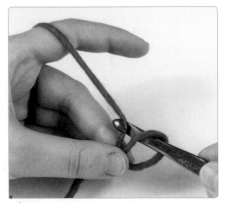

2 Create the knot. Put the hook through the loop and grab the working yarn with the hook. Pull it through the loop. As you can see, the working yarn is usually held by the fingers of your non-dominant hand while you stitch. Your thumb and a finger pinch the tail of the yarn and the stitches just made, and the index or middle finger give the yarn some tension so there isn't slack between the hook and your finger. The pinkie and ring fingers act as brakes to release the yarn gradually and create more tension.

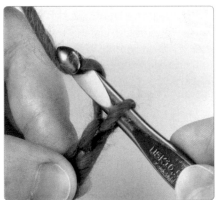

3 Start the chain. The hook shaft should now have the loop of yarn on it at all times to prevent work from unraveling. Put the hook through the loop, wrap the working yarn over the hook from behind and down over the top of the hook throat, grab the yarn with the hook, and pull the yarn through the loop on the hook.

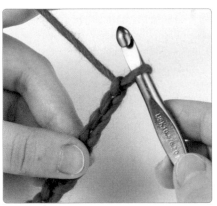

4 Continue the chain. Continue wrapping the working yarn over the hook from behind and down over the top of the hook throat, and grabbing the yarn and pulling it through the loop on the hook shaft. Each time you pull a yarn-over through the loop, you have made a chain stitch (ch). Continue making this chain for as many times as the pattern states in the instructions for the foundation chain. The little knot at the base of the first chain does not count as a stitch and neither does the "live" loop that is on the hook. You count the number "V" shaped stitches—each one is a chain.

CONTINUING WITH SINGLE CROCHET

5 **Turn your work and start a new row.** To begin the row after the foundation chain, you begin by making a "single crochet" stitch in the second chain stitch from the hook. When you look at the chain placed horizontally on a surface, the little "V"-shapes of the chain are lying down with the bottom point of each "V" pointing away from the hook. Insert the hook into the top strand of the second chain stitch.

6 **Hook the yarn.** Wrap the yarn over the hook's throat from behind and down over and grab the yarn with the hook's head and pull it under that strand only. You should now have two loops on the hook's shaft. Now wrap the working yarn over the hook from behind, grab it with the hook's nose, and pull it through both loops already on the hook. This creates one single crochet (sc) stitch

7 **Continue the crochet.** At the end of the row, chain one stitch, then turn your work to go back across the stitches just made. You will insert your hook under both strands of the "V", not just under one as you did when you inserted the hook into a chain. Now that you are working into other single crochet stitches (sts), you need a firm fabric, so it is standard to go under both strands with the hook. Then finish the single crochet stitch as above with a yarn over, pull through fabric, then yarn over and pull through both loops on hook. Repeat this the given number of times.

JEWELRY AND ACCESSORIES

DIFFICULTY: Noob

MAKES: Earrings, necklace, pin, keychain, or magnet

Because Perler beads mimic the look of Minecraft so well, I realized that I could easily use game graphics to create a ton of fun trinkets like necklaces, earrings, pins, keychains, and magnets. All I needed was a few findings to get started and maybe a bit of glue. You can also try out mini beads to make jewelry that's both striking and dainty.

MATERIALS AND TOOLS:

- Pattern(s) (page 55)
- Perler beads in colors to match selected pattern
- Earring hooks, necklace chain, magnet, keychain, or flat pin back
- Metal jump rings (for necklace, earrings, or keychain)
- Hot glue gun (for magnet or pin)
- Perler bead peg board
- Iron
- Ironing paper
- Jewelry pliers (for necklace, earrings, or keychain)

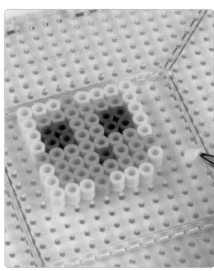

1 Assemble the beads. Following the technique on page 20, assemble and iron Perler beads following the pattern of your choice (page 55). For earrings, make sure to assemble a pair.

2 Create the earrings. Using jewelry pliers, open and loop a jump ring through the topmost bead of each earring. Loop an earring hook onto each jump ring and close them back up to complete.

3 Create the necklace. Using jewelry pliers, open and loop a jump ring onto the topmost bead. Loop a necklace chain through the ring and close it back up to complete.

4 Create the keychain. Using jewelry pliers, open and loop a jump ring onto the topmost bead. Loop the ring of a keychain into the jump ring and close it back up to complete.

5 **Create the pin.** For a pin, use hot glue to adhere a pin back to the back of the Perler bead piece. Allow the glue to dry fully before using.

6 **Create the magnet.** For a magnet, use hot glue to adhere a magnet to the back of the Perler bead piece. Allow the glue to dry fully before using.

PIXEL PLANT

DIFFICULTY: Level+1   **MAKES:** One 7" (17.5cm) high potted plant

Did you know that you can build your own garden in Minecraft? In the game, different colored flowers are used for making dyes or just for brightening up your home. I love planting flowers in the game, so I knew I had to figure out a way to craft them in real life. With a few Perler beads and some flowerpots, I made my own pixel garden! These plants look perfect on a desk or even a windowsill for a cheerful bit of greenery that will never wilt!

MATERIALS AND TOOLS:

- Pattern(s) (page 56)
- 3" (7cm) high terra cotta flowerpot
- Perler beads in colors to match selected pattern, plus lots of brown
- 4" (11cm) cube of floral foam
- Acrylic paint in brown and green
- 5" (13cm) square of brown felt
- Hot glue gun
- Perler bead peg board
- Iron
- Ironing paper
- Craft knife/scissors
- Kitchen knife
- Paintbrushes

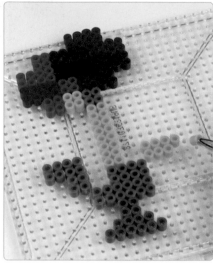

1 Assemble the beads. Following the technique on page 20, assemble and iron a Perler bead flower following one of the patterns on page 56. For especially tall flowers, you'll need a larger peg board.

2 Paint the pot. For an added bit of color, paint the pot green along the rim and brown on the bottom.

4 Insert the plant. Insert the brown root part of the plant into the slit cut in the top of the foam. Check to make sure it fits snugly and that the slit is deep enough, then remove it for the next step.

5 Create the flower base. Trim the brown felt so it fits on top of the foam. Cut a slit that matches the one in the foam, then glue the felt on top of the foam so the openings match up. Apply hot glue into the opening, then insert the flower, holding it until the glue dries.

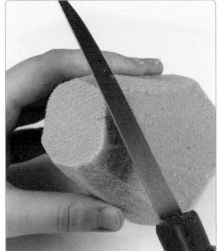

3 **Carve the foam.** Using a craft knife or kitchen knife, carve the floral foam so it fits inside the pot snugly. (Children should get an adult's help with this step.) Cut a 1½″ (4cm) long and deep slit in the top for the plant. Apply hot glue along the bottom and sides of the foam and press it into the pot. Allow it to cool.

6 **Add the pixel dirt.** For a final touch, spread brown Perler beads over the felt to create pixel "dirt."

●● **GAMER TIP** ●●

TYPES OF TOOLS

Use the proper tools when collecting items in the Minecraft world. Using the wrong tool will make it break faster than if you were using the correct one. Use shovels for dirt, sand, and gravel, axes for trees and leaves, and pickaxes for stone, ore, and other hard materials. Or go straight to the TNT for instant results!

PERLER BEAD COIN BOX

DIFFICULTY: Level+1   **MAKES:** One 4" x 4" x 4" (10 x 10 x 10cm) box

Step up your Perler bead game and go 3-D! This interesting project takes flat pieces of fused Perler beads and assembles them to make a 3-D box. I decided to make the classic chest that's used in the Minecraft world for storing items. By including a hole in the top, I designed the box for my spare change, which I could easily retrieve by opening up the lid.

....

MATERIALS AND TOOLS:

- Pattern(s) (page 57)
- Perler beads in black, medium brown, and dark brown
- 2" x 4" (5 x 10cm) piece of black felt
- Hot glue gun
- Perler bead peg board
- Iron
- Ironing paper

♥♥♥ **GAMER INSIDER**

BUILDING A COUNTRY

Members of the Danish Geodata Agency recreated the entire country of Denmark in the game, using public data about landscapes, roads, and more to make it as true-to-life as possible. The result is the first country that anyone can visit in the game in a 1:1 ratio; it is comprised of about 4000 billion blocks. This is just one of the most impressive things that players have done in a long list of recreated real-world landmarks, cities, buildings, and more from the present day as well as the past.

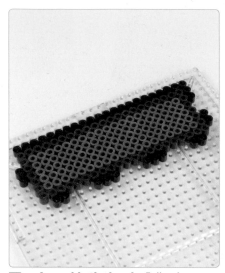

1 Assemble the beads. Following the technique on page 20, assemble and iron the pieces of the coin box following the patterns on page 57. Be sure not to flatten the beads too much when you iron the pieces, or they won't fit together correctly.

2 Assemble the bottom. Assemble the bottom of the box by linking together the slots found in the sides of the box pieces. Four bottom side pieces should link up vertically around the bottom piece. For security, use dabs of hot glue to hold the joints together.

3 Assemble the top. Similar to the bottom, assemble the top pieces by linking together the top side pieces around the top piece (which has the coin slot). Use more hot glue to keep the joints stable.

4 Add the inner ridge. Assemble the inner ridge pieces similarly to the top and bottom side edges by joining them at the corners. Tuck the ridge halfway into the top of the box and glue it in place with hot glue.

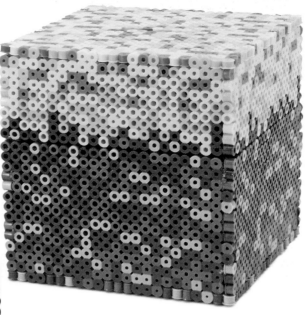

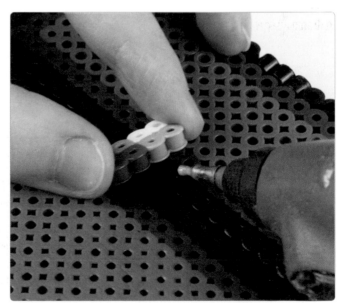

5 **Add the hinge.** Rest the box top onto the bottom and place the box face down on the work surface. Using hot glue, adhere the piece of felt to the back, centered over the line where the top and bottom meet. This creates the hinge of the box.

6 **Add the latch.** Glue the top half of the latch to the center front of the box. Attach it to the top half of the box only.

DUCT TAPE WALLET

DIFFICULTY: Level+2   **MAKES:** One 4¼" x 3¼" (11 x 8.5cm) wallet

I figured out a way to carry my favorite Minecraft character with me everywhere I go with this classic duct tape wallet. The handy wallet holds bills, cards, and a photo ID, while also sporting one of many Minecraft character faces available in the pattern section on page 58.

MATERIALS AND TOOLS:

- Pattern(s) (page 58)
- Duct tape in 2 or more colors
- Parchment paper
- 4" x 2½" (10 x 6.5cm) rectangle of clear plastic (such as report cover plastic)
- Craft knife/scissors
- Ruler
- Cutting mat

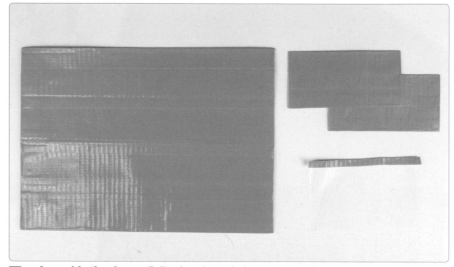

1 **Assemble the sheets.** Following the technique on page 21, create double-sided duct tape sheets in the following sizes: main wallet, 9" x 6½" (23 x 16.5cm) (1); card pockets, 4" x 2" (10 x 5cm) (2). Also edge one long side of the clear plastic with a ⅝" (1.5cm) wide strip of duct tape.

♥♥♥ GAMER INSIDER

GREAT BEGINNINGS

The Internet message board history of the inception of Minecraft is an interesting one. The creator, Swedish programmer Markus "Notch" Persson, posted the earliest version of the game online and received such responses as "I hope you make something really good of this, dude; I think it has a lot of potential" and "That's pretty cool. I just dig around in the ground a bit, and suddenly I'm in this underground cave! Great sense of exploration already." The first screenshot ever shared of gameplay featured a simple single-block-wide bridge.

2 **Fold the wallet.** Measure in 3⅛" (8cm) from one long side of the large rectangle and fold along this line. One half should be a little shorter than the other—this forms the bill slot for the main wallet.

3 **Add the card pockets.** Align one card pocket on the left side of the wallet, 1" (2.5cm) down from the top edge. Tape it in place with a strip of duct tape along the bottom. Place the next card pocket on top of it, shifted ½" (1.5cm) down, and tape it in place along the bottom in the same manner.

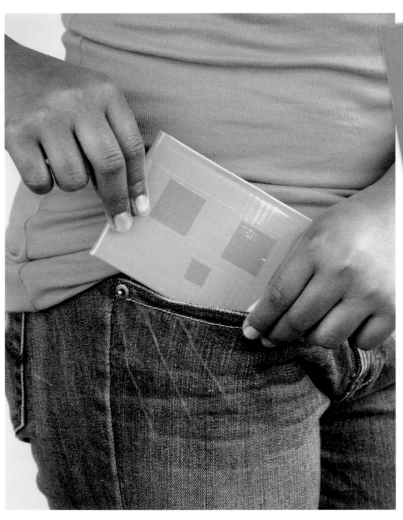

4 **Add the ID pocket.** Align the clear pocket on the right side of the wallet and tape it in place along the bottom the same way as you did the card pockets.

5 **Tape the sides.** Use more strips of duct tape to tape the sides of all the pockets. On the far right and far left, wrap the tape around to the front of the wallet. This will also join the sides of the wallet's bill slot.

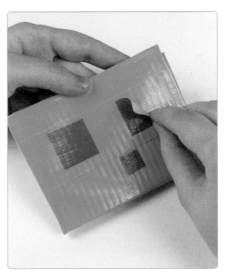

6 **Add the design.** Following the technique on page 21, trace one of the patterns on page 58 to make a sticker. Fold the wallet in half with the pockets facing inward and add the sticker to the outside, creating the character face.

FOAM TOOLS

DIFFICULTY: Level+2

MAKES: One 22½" x 11½" x 1" (57 x 29 x 2.5cm) foam sword or one 17" x 13" x 1" (43 x 33 x 2.5cm) foam pickaxe

Pickaxes, swords, shovels, and axes are the basic tools that get you started in Minecraft. Finally finding diamonds to make a diamond sword or pickaxe is a feat unto itself. But I wanted to make my own without all that mining! Here's a design to make one that just uses some duct tape and craft foam slab/roll (a heavy duty foam often used for cushioning projects, chair pads, and camper cushions). Tape-covered foam makes for a weapon that is sturdy enough to wield but soft enough for play-fighting.

MATERIALS AND TOOLS:

- Pattern(s) (page 59)
- 16" x 16" (40.5 x 40.5cm) square sheet of drawing paper
- Craft foam slab/roll (1" [2.5cm] wide): 24" x 12" (61 x 30.5cm) rectangle for sword; 19" x 15" (48.5 x 38cm) rectangle for pickaxe
- Duct tape in black, brown, and other colors to match the chosen tool material
- Cutting mat
- Craft knife/scissors
- Ruler

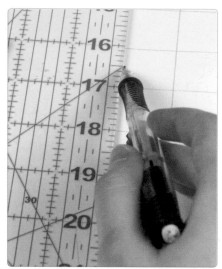

1 **Create the pattern.** Draw a 1" x 1" (2.5 x 2.5cm) grid across the pattern paper, creating a grid of 16 squares by 16 squares. Using the sword or pickaxe pattern on page 59, outline the shape of the tool on the squares and cut out the shape to use as a pattern.

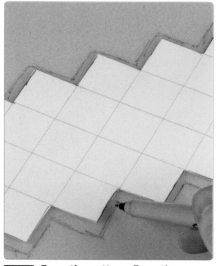

2 **Trace the pattern.** Trace the paper pattern onto the craft foam with about ¼" (0.5cm) of breathing room, because the foam will be a little compressed when wrapped in duct tape. When complete, cut the shape out of the craft foam.

3 **Cover the base.** Use strips of black duct tape to completely cover the foam, creating the base color.

4 **Add the pixels.** Cut 1" x 1" (2.5 x 2.5cm) squares from the other duct tape colors and place them over the black, following the colors and placement from the pattern. Be sure to cover both sides with pixels.

Foam diamond sword

Foam iron pickaxe

END-OF-THE-ROLL BOX

DIFFICULTY: Level+2   **MAKES:** One 3" x 3" x 2" (7.5 x 7.5 x 5cm) box

After making all the duct tape projects in this book, I ended up with some empty duct tape rolls. So I put them to good use by making these handy round boxes with matching lids! You can decorate them with the faces of Minecraft characters and use them to hold desk items, toys, or to sort your Perler bead collection.

....

MATERIALS AND TOOLS:

- Pattern(s) (page 58)
- 2 empty duct tape rolls
- Duct tape in 2 or more colors
- Parchment paper
- 7" x 4" (18 x 10cm) piece of heavy cardboard
- Craft knife/scissors
- Ruler
- Cutting mat

1 **Cut open the bottom.** Mark a ⅞" (2.5cm) wide space going across one of the duct tape rolls. Using scissors, cut away this section. Then close up the opening with strips of duct tape. This roll will be the box bottom; the other will be the lid.

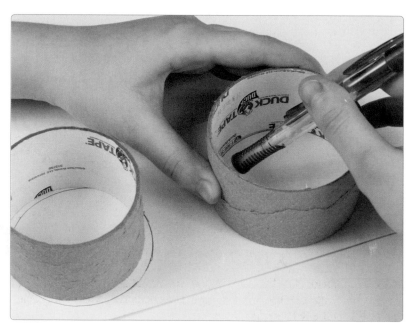

2 **Trace the top and bottom.** Using the cardboard, trace the outside of the bottom piece and the inside of the lid piece. Cut out the pieces of cardboard and keep them with their corresponding halves.

●● GAMER TIP ●●

SAVE YOUR SHOVEL

Tired of crafting shovels? Take out the bottom block of a stack of sand or gravel with your shovel and quickly replace it with a torch, then watch the torch do all the work.

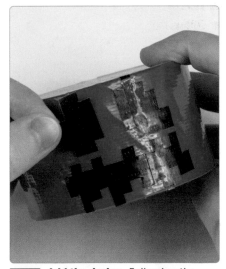

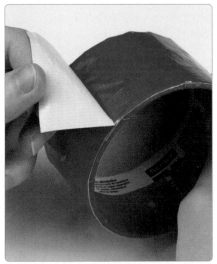

3 **Install the cardboard.** Place the cardboard for the box bottom over the empty bottom roll and tape it in place to hold it. Repeat this for the box lid, taping the cardboard in place so it rests just inside the top edge of the roll.

4 **Cover both halves.** Completely cover both box halves in duct tape.

5 **Add the design.** Following the technique on page 21, trace one of the patterns on page 58 to make a sticker. Apply it to the lid of the box so it faces outward when the box lid and bottom are brought together.

CARDBOARD COSTUME HEAD

DIFFICULTY: Level+3   **MAKES:** One costume head sized to fit

Have a Halloween party to attend and need a quick costume? Or maybe you just want to roam your backyard feeling like Steve, like I did. Either way, this cardboard head looks just like the beloved Steve character from Minecraft. The added cap inside makes it comfortable to wear, too. I had so much fun wearing the head myself! You can be Steve like I was or switch out the colors to make it completely custom!

....

MATERIALS AND TOOLS:

- ■ Pattern (page 59)
- ■ Scrapbook paper in shades of brown, tan, peach, white, and blue
- ■ Box sized to fit comfortably around your head
- ■ Decoupage medium (optional; see step 4)
- ■ Snugly-fitting cap (such as a baseball cap)
- ■ Acrylic paint in peach or light pink
- ■ Hot glue gun
- ■ Rubber cement
- ■ Craft knife/scissors
- ■ Ruler
- ■ Cutting mat
- ■ Paintbrush

1 Prep the box. Make sure the box is fully assembled and is flat on each side with one side completely open for your head. To make step 4 more forgiving, give the box a coat of peach paint.

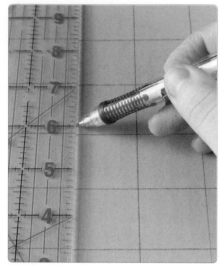

2 Grid out the box. Using a ruler, draw a grid on each side of the box that is 8 units by 8 units.

3 Cut the eye holes. Following the pattern on page 59, mark where each color goes in each square. Using the craft knife, cut out the eye holes. If needed, try on the box to be sure the eye holes match up with your own eye line.

Rubber Cement Tip

Surprisingly, the easiest way to use rubber cement is usually not listed on the jar! For a strong hold that's also repositionable, try applying the glue to both the paper and the box. Allow the glue to dry for 10 seconds or so; the glue should go from shiny to matte. Apply the pieces at this time and they should stick instantly. Don't be afraid to spread the glue all over for good coverage, because you can rub the excess away with your finger or a rubber cement eraser.

PROJECTS

Front **Right** **Back**

Left **Top** **Inside**

4 **Apply the paper.** Cut squares from scrapbook paper to fit the grid squares. Glue the squares in place with rubber cement based on the placement of the colors in the pattern. When complete, consider giving the head a brush of decoupage medium to seal everything.

5 **Install the hat.** Hot glue the top of the hat to the inside top of the box with the front of the hat facing the front of the box. Depending on the size of the box, you may want to bend the brim of the hat out of the way.

FLASHLIGHT TORCH

DIFFICULTY: Level+3   **MAKES:** One box to hold a 10" (25.5cm) Maglite flashlight

Torches are one of the most valuable and frequently used items in Minecraft—they keep many monsters at bay and light your way through the various underground caves and ravines you'll find in your world. I made one of my own fully functional torches with a basic 10" (25.5cm) Maglite so I could bring it with me on loads of dark and mysterious adventures. Feel free to use other flashlights for this project; you'll just need to adjust the size of the box accordingly.

MATERIALS AND TOOLS:

- Pattern (page 60)
- 10" (25.5cm) Maglite flashlight
- 10" x 13" (25.5 x 33cm) rectangle of cardboard
- Scrapbook paper in light, medium, and dark brown, orange, yellow, and cream
- 4¼" x 4¼" (11 x 11cm) square of clear vinyl
- Clear tape
- Rubber cement
- 1" (3cm) of adhesive hook-and-loop tape
- Decoupage medium (optional; see step 4)
- Ruler
- Pencil
- Craft knife/scissors
- Hot glue gun
- Bone folder

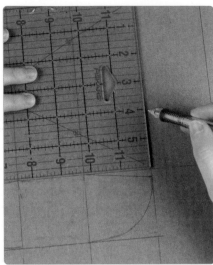

1 Draft the box pattern. Using a ruler and pencil, draw out the box pattern onto the cardboard from the measurements and instructions on page 60. When finished, cut out the box and score all the lines with the bone folder. Also cut out the hole for the on/off switch.

2 Assemble the box. Construct the box by folding it along the scored lines, then joining the long flap to the opposite end of the box. Glue it in place with hot glue.

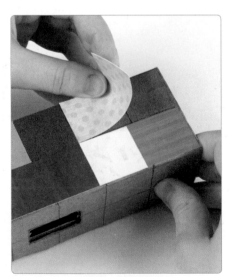

4 Add the paper pixels. From the scrapbook paper, cut several 1⅛" (3cm) paper squares to fit over each grid square, matching the colors up with those found on the pattern. Glue the squares in place with rubber cement. When complete, consider applying several coats of decoupage medium for a permanent hold.

5 Add the vinyl top. Cut 1" (2.5cm) squares from each corner of the vinyl square, then place the vinyl over the open top of the box. Fold the sides down and tape the vinyl in place with clear tape.

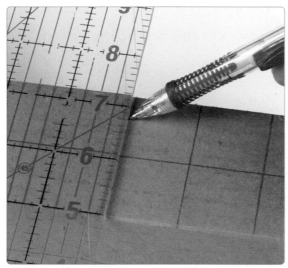

3 **Grid out the box.** Draw a grid across all sides of the box, 2 squares wide by 9 squares tall or 1⅛" (3cm) squares.

6 **Add the hook-and-loop tape.** Close up the box by folding in the side flaps and tucking them inside. Add the adhesive hook-and-loop tape where the front and back flap meet so that the bottom of the box is strong but opens for removal of the flashlight later.

ORE LIGHT

One of the most arduous but rewarding aspects of Minecraft is mining for special ores, such as diamonds, redstone, and glowstone. While mining through layers and layers of stone, you'll know you've succeeded in finding these special ores when you stumble upon their distinctive glow—a glow that I mimicked here with these fun decorative lights! With a basic cardboard box and a wireless light (such as a touch light), I created a decorative desk light and nightlight to cast a comforting blue, red, or yellow glow on my room. Make your favorite!

MATERIALS AND TOOLS:

- Pattern(s) (page 61)
- Wireless light
- Box sized to cover your wireless light
- Scrapbook paper in four shades of gray (diamond or redstone) or brown (glowstone)
- Transparent plastic sheeting in blue, red, or yellow: enough to cover 5 sides of your box
- Acrylic paint in gray
- Rubber cement
- Duct tape
- Decoupage medium (optional; see step 4)
- Ruler
- Craft knife/scissors
- Paintbrush

1 **Paint the box.** Assemble or trim the box so it has five complete sides with one open side. With the gray paint, paint the entire box so any small mistakes you might make in step 4 aren't noticeable.

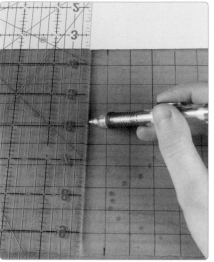

2 **Grid out the box.** Draw a grid out on the box of 10 units by 10 units along each of the five sides.

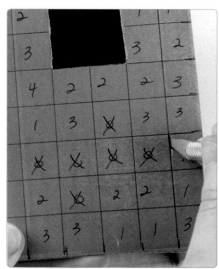

3 **Cut out the holes.** Label each square with a number corresponding to the color found in the pattern on page 61. Cut the blue/red/yellow sections out with the craft knife.

4 **Add the paper pixels.** From the scrapbook paper, cut several squares that fit the grid and paste them in place with rubber cement by color according to the pattern. When finished, consider applying several coats of decoupage medium for a permanent finish.

5 **Add the plastic.** Cut 5 squares from the colored plastic that measure about ½" (1cm) smaller than the sides of the box. Tape them in place with strips of duct tape on the inside of each side of the box.

MINING ORE

Diamond ore

One of the rarest kinds of ore that, when mined, drops 1 diamond. Diamonds can be used to create the most durable armor and tools in the game.

Redstone ore

A type of ore that, when mined, drops 4–5 redstones. This ingredient can be used as a conduit to power and craft electrical items, such as redstone torches, pistons, and clocks.

Glowstone

A special kind of block found in the Nether realm of the game. The blocks produce light that is brighter than a torch, so it's helpful to use when building your Overworld home.

BUILDING BLOCKS

DIFFICULTY: Level+1   **MAKES:** 2" (5cm) cube blocks in 9 different terrains

With all my other Minecraft goodies around, I didn't want to skip the basic building blocks of the game. Using just a few wood blocks and some copies printed from this book, I created all the stone, wood, brick, or dirt blocks I needed to build a real mini Minecraft world. Build a house just like ones you've made in the game, or make a home for all of your other wonderful creations.

MATERIALS AND TOOLS:

- Pattern(s) (pages 61–62)
- 2" (5cm) unfinished wood blocks
- Printout of block patterns
- Decoupage medium
- Parchment paper
- Rubber cement
- Craft knife/scissors
- Paintbrush

1 Print the block pieces. Copy the block side patterns found on pages 61–62; six squares are needed for each block. Note how many copies of the pattern page you'll need to supply all six, because certain terrains might have different images on each side.

2 Apply the block sides. Cut out the printed pieces needed for all six sides of the blocks. Using rubber cement, glue them to the wood blocks according to the notes on the pattern page (top, bottom, sides, etc.). Be sure that the top and bottom are opposite each other and each side block is facing top side up.

3 Decoupage the surface. To prevent the edges of the paper from peeling, apply several coats of decoupage medium to the surface of each block. Allow the blocks to dry on parchment paper between coats to prevent sticking.

PAINTED WALL ART

DIFFICULTY: Level+2   **MAKES:** One painted canvas in size of your choice

I covered my room in Minecraft décor with these easy painted canvases! By utilizing the pixelated nature of the game, you can quickly create all your favorite characters by just painting inside the lines. Accent your favorite gaming area or cover a whole wall in a grid of Minecraft awesomeness, like I did.

MATERIALS AND TOOLS:

- Pattern(s) (pages 55 and 59)
- Square canvas
- Acrylic paints
- Painter's tape (optional; see step 3)
- Ruler
- Paintbrushes

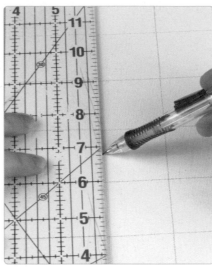

1 **Grid out the canvas.** Choose a pattern from pages 55 or 59 and draw out a grid on the canvas equal to the squares found in the pattern.

2 **Number the squares.** Label each square with the corresponding color following the pattern. For ease, consider defining each color by a number, creating a paint-by-number canvas.

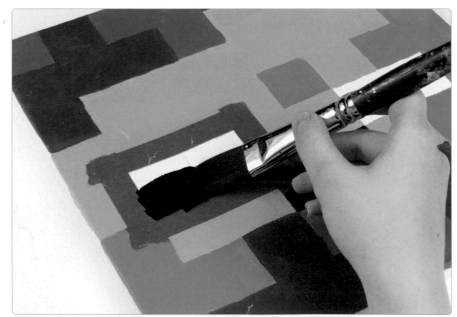

3 **Paint the squares.** Follow the gridded pattern to paint each square with the corresponding paint color. If you're concerned about neatness, use painter's tape when painting each section, being sure to let the surrounding paint dry before sticking on the tape.

SCREEN PRINTED ACCESSORIES

DIFFICULTY: Level+2

MAKES: One screen printed item of any size

I wanted to make something I could proudly display in public, so I decided to screen print some shirts! With just a simple painting technique using freezer paper, you can decorate all of your favorite clothes and accessories in Minecraft style. This method works wonders on any fabric surface, such as tote bags, hoodies, shoes, and most definitely t-shirts. In an afternoon you can easily create a load of Minecraft-themed goodies for parties or gifts.

··

MATERIALS AND TOOLS:

- Pattern(s) (page 58)
- Fabric item for screen printing
- Freezer paper
- Fabric paints in colors of your desired character
- Scrap paper
- Craft knife/scissors
- Ruler
- Cutting mat
- Iron
- Washable fabric marker (optional; see step 3)

1 Grid out the paper. Draw a square on the paper (matte) side of the freezer paper that is the size you want the image. Draw a grid inside the square with a ruler equal to the number of squares in one of the patterns on page 58.

2 Outline and cut out the pattern. Following the pattern, draw the outline of the character face onto the grid. Then, using scissors or a craft knife, cut out the outline.

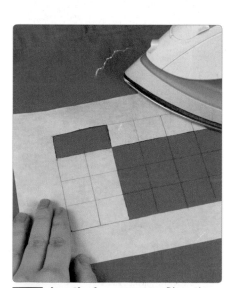

3 Iron the freezer paper. Place the freezer paper on the fabric item, shiny side down, and iron it in place with medium heat and no steam. When the paper adheres, you're ready for painting. If your chosen pattern has multiple colors, draw a grid inside the open area with a fabric marker.

4 Paint the outline. For insurance, put some scrap paper inside and beneath the fabric project in case the paint bleeds. Paint in the open area of the freezer paper, using appropriate colors within each gridline. When complete, carefully peel off the paper while the paint is still wet.

Paint-by-Number Shoes

These Enderman shoes were made the same way as the Painted Wall Art project (page 44). To make a pair, grid out the tops of the shoes with a fabric pencil, then fill in the squares with fabric paints matching the pattern on page 55.

NO-SEW FLEECE QUILT

DIFFICULTY: Level+1   **MAKES:** One 64" x 64" (162 x 162cm) quilt

Did you know that you can make a full quilt without any sewing at all? By using versatile fleece, I tied all of my seams together to create a colorful patchwork quilt. The blocks adapt to pixel patterns wonderfully, so in the end I had a gorgeous blanket that looked like my favorite Minecraft character, the Creeper. Using different colors, you could make a blanket from any of the other patterns on page 55 as well.

MATERIALS AND TOOLS:

- Pattern (page 55)
- 2 yd. (2m) black fleece
- 1¼ yd. (1.25m) each of fleece in four different shades of green
- Fabric scissors
- Washable fabric marker
- Ruler
- Cutting mat and rotary cutter (optional; see step 1)

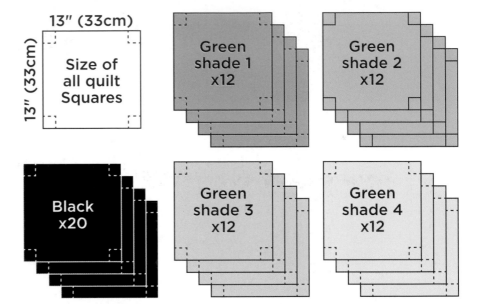

13" (33cm) / 13" (33cm) — Size of all quilt Squares

Green shade 1 x12

Green shade 2 x12

Black x20

Green shade 3 x12

Green shade 4 x12

♥♥♥ GAMER INSIDER

VIRTUAL UH-REALITY

Minecraft's creator, Markus "Notch" Persson, was in talks about possibly bringing Minecraft to the virtual reality headset Oculus Rift, but decided against it when Facebook bought Oculus Rift, saying, "Facebook creeps me out." So fans of the game might have to wait a long time for a virtual reality version of the game.

1 **Cut out the squares.** Cut out twenty 13" x 13" (33 x 33cm) squares of the black fleece and twelve 13" x 13" (33 x 33cm) squares from each of the four shades of green fleece. Use fabric scissors or a combination of a rotary cutter, cutting mat, and ruler to make it go faster.

2 **Measure the fringe area.** Using a ruler and fabric marker, draw 2½" (6.5cm) wide borders around the edge of each square. Cut away the corner sections where the borders cross.

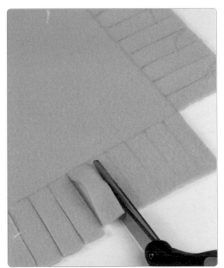

3 **Cut the fringe.** On each square, cut slits spaced ¾" (2cm) apart up to the border line on all four sides, creating fringe.

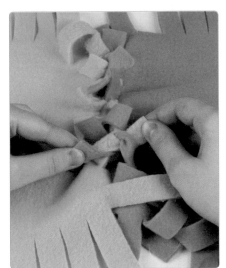

4 Tie the blocks. Following the pattern on page 55, place two adjacent blocks side by side matching up the fringe pieces. Tie corresponding pieces of fringe from each block into a square knot. Do this along the entire seam of the squares, being sure that the fringe matches up evenly along the way.

5 Tie the rows. Continue in this manner, tying one block to another while following the pattern. Tie up one row at a time, and, when all the rows are complete, tie all the rows together.

6 Tie the edges. When all the rows have been tied together, make knots from the fringe around the edges of the entire quilt to finish it.

FELT PLUSH CUBE

DIFFICULTY: Level+3   **MAKES:** One 4½" x 4½" x 4½" (11.5 x 11.5 x 11.5cm) plush

I wanted to come up with a project that was a fun way to learn hand sewing, so I decided easy cube plushes would be perfect! Learn a simple whipstitch and use it to make a plush version of your favorite Minecraft character. You can make mobs that are already cubes, such as the Slime or Magma Cube, or make a whole collection of cube-ified creatures. They're perfect for stacking or using to inhabit your handmade Minecraft world.

MATERIALS AND TOOLS:

- Pattern(s) (page 58)
- For beginner practice: two 4½" x 4½" (11.5 x 11.5cm) squares of scrap felt
- Six 4½" x 4½" (11.5 x 11.5cm) squares of felt in a color to match your character
- 3" x 3" (7.5 x 7.5cm) piece of coordinating felt
- Fabric glue
- Matching thread
- Batting
- Sewing needle
- Fabric scissors
- Ruler

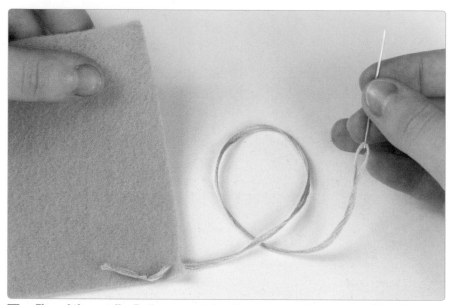

1 **Thread the needle.** To those new to hand sewing, practice steps 1 and 2 with scraps before proceeding. Begin by threading the needle with a length of thread about twice as long as your arm. Knot the two ends together and pull the needle to the middle. Bring the needle through one corner of a scrap piece of fabric, about ⅛" (0.5cm) from the edge, and pull it taut.

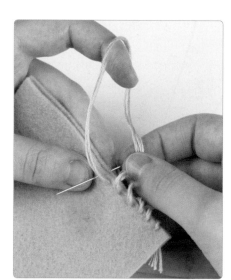

2 **Learn the whipstitch.** All the seams in this project are sewn using a whipstitch. This is a stitch where you bring the needle straight through two layers of fabric from back to front, going down the length of the seam. The finished seam will be wrapped in thread. The two layers are stitched in this manner, moving across the edge about ⅛" (0.5cm) each time.

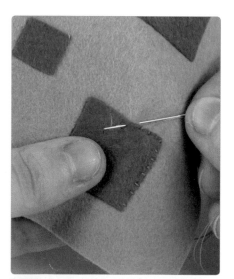

3 **Apply the face.** Use one of the face patterns on page 58 to trace and cut a face from the felt. Use the fabric glue to glue it in place in the middle of one of the squares. For extra security, you might want to sew around the edge of the face as well, using the whipstitch.

●● GAMER TIP ●●

HUNTING FOR DIAMONDS

Diamond ore can only be found between layers 1 through 16 of a world, and is mostly found around layer 12. Use a map to dig down to Y=12 for the best chance to fetch some diamonds.

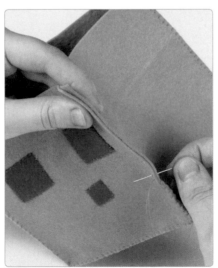

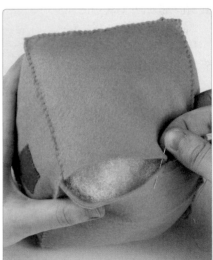

4 **Sew the bottom.** Match up the bottom edge of the face square with the side of another square (this will become the bottom). Layer them with the face facing outward and do a whipstitch across that edge. Repeat this with the other sides of the bottom and three more side squares.

5 **Sew the sides.** Bring up the sides of the cube and sew a whipstitch where the edges of the sides meet up.

6 **Sew the top.** Place the last square on top of the cube and sew a whipstitch around the perimeter. Before you reach the end, stuff the cube with batting, then finish up the seam.

CROCHETED CREEPER

DIFFICULTY: Level MAX   **MAKES:** 14" x 6" x 6" (35.5 x 15.5 x 15.5cm) plush

I love cuddly creatures, so I just had to make the iconic Creeper in a size that's big enough for me to hug! Using bulky yarn and the crochet primer on page 22, this project is perfect for beginners to crochet. It's constructed from simple squares and cubes just like the Felt Plush Cube project on page 50, so it's easy to put together. Just be careful if you start to hear your Creeper hiss!

MATERIALS AND TOOLS:

- Pattern (page 58)
- About 300 yd. (300m) of super bulky weight yarn in green (see below for specific brands)
- About 2 yd. (2m) of worsted weight black yarn
- 4" x 4" (10 x 10cm) square of black felt
- Fabric glue
- Batting
- Crochet hook, size M/13 (00)
- Yarn needle

YARN USED:

- Large light green Creeper: Lion Brand® Yarn, Hometown USA® (5oz./81yd. [142g/74m]), 4 skeins #172 Oklahoma City Green. Hook used: size K [7mm].
- Medium dark green Creeper: Lion Brand® Yarn, Homespun® (6oz./185yd. [170g/169m]), 1 skein #604 Forest. Hook used: size I [5.5mm].
- Small metallic Creeper: Patons® Yarn, Metallic™ (3oz./252yd. [85g/230m]), 1 skein #95244 Metallic Green (about 150 yd. [137m] used). Hook used: size E [3.5mm].

CROCHETING THE PIECES

Head sides: make 6

1. **Row 1:** Make a foundation chain of 11 stitches.

2. **Row 2:** Work a single crochet (sc) stitch in the 2nd chain from the hook and then a sc in each of the remaining 9 chains for a total of 10 sc, turn the work.

3. **Rows 3–12:** Ch 1, sc in each stitch (st) across, turn. After the twelfth row, cut the yarn leaving an 8" (20cm) tail and pull on the loop that's on the hook till the yarn end comes through. Tighten gently.

Body front/back: make 2

4. **Row 1:** Make a foundation chain of 11 stitches.

5. **Row 2:** Work a sc stitch in the 2nd chain from the hook and then a sc in each of the remaining 9 chains for a total of 10 sc, turn the work.

6. **Rows 3–18:** Ch 1, sc in each st across, turn. After the eighteenth row, cut the yarn leaving a 12" (30cm) tail and pull on the loop that's on the hook till the yarn end comes through. Tighten gently.

Body sides: make 2

7. **Row 1:** Make a foundation chain of 6 stitches.

8. **Row 2:** Work a sc stitch in the 2nd chain from the hook and then a sc in each of the remaining 4 chains for a total of 5 sc, turn the work.

9. **Rows 3–18:** Ch 1, sc in each st across, turn. After the eighteenth row, cut the yarn leaving a 12" (30cm) tail and pull on the loop that's on the hook till the yarn end comes through. Tighten gently.

Body top/bottom: make 2

10. **Row 1:** Make a foundation chain of 11 stitches.

11. **Row 2:** Work a sc stitch in the 2nd chain from the hook and then a sc in each of the remaining 9 chains for a total of 10 sc, turn the work.

12. **Rows 3–6:** Ch 1, sc in each st across, turn. After the sixth row, cut the yarn leaving a 6" (15cm) tail and pull on the loop that's on the hook till the yarn end comes through. Tighten gently.

Feet sides: make 16

13   **Row 1:** Make a foundation chain of 6 stitches.

14   **Row 2:** Work a sc stitch in the 2nd chain from the hook and then a sc in each of the remaining 4 chains for a total of 5 sc, turn the work.

15   **Rows 3–9:** Ch 1, sc in each st across, turn. After the ninth row, cut the yarn leaving a 6″ (15cm) tail and pull on the loop that's on the hook till the yarn end comes through. Tighten gently.

Feet top/bottom: make 8

16   **Row 1:** Make a foundation chain of 6 stitches.

17   **Row 2:** Work a sc stitch in the 2nd chain from the hook and then a sc in each of the remaining 4 chains for a total of 5 sc, turn the work.

18   **Rows 3–6:** Ch 1, sc in each st across, turn. After the sixth row, cut the yarn leaving a 6″ (15cm) tail and pull on the loop that's on the hook till the yarn end comes through. Tighten gently.

Instructions continue on page 54.

●● GAMER TIP ●●

AWESOME SEEDS

A seed in Minecraft is essentially a special code for generating a pre-built world. These worlds can have mountainous terrains, desert islands, labyrinth-like cave systems, or ore-rich landscapes. The fun seeds below are case-sensitive, so be sure to type them exactly as they appear!

gargamel
Spawn in a dark cave surrounded by giant cliffs.

england
Spawn next to a jungle temple.

-671258039
Visit a desert temple with an abandoned mineshaft.

Artomix
Try to survive on a tiny island.

Diamonds, diamonds everywhere!
There just might be some diamonds around.

ASSEMBLING THE CREEPER

1 Apply the face. Use the face pattern on page 58 to trace and cut a face from the felt fabric. See step 3 of the Felt Plush Cube project (page 50) and use fabric glue to glue the felt Creeper face centered on one of the head sides. If you need the face to be larger to fit the square, follow steps 1–3 of the Screen Printed Accessories project (page 46) to make a paper pattern to fit.

2 Create the cubes. Gather the six pieces for the Creeper body: 2 sides, 2 front/back, and 2 top/bottom. See steps 4–6 of the Felt Plush Cube project (page 51) and assemble the pieces into one complete body. Make sure the sides are sewn around the bottom piece with the top added last. Use the thread tails and the yarn needle to stitch the sides using a whipstitch.

3 Finish the remaining pieces. Repeat step 2 with the head and feet pieces. When finished, you should have 1 head, 1 body, and 4 feet assembled.

4 Attach the head. Center the head on top of the body and stitch it in place around the top edge of the body.

5 Sew the feet. Align the top edge of the feet with the bottom edge of the body. Sew two in a row on the front of the body and two in a row on the back. For extra stability, sew the feet in place where they meet the front of the body and again where they meet the underside of the body.

6 Make the toes. Using the black yarn, stitch several big whip stitches along the bottom edge of the feet to create toes.

Jewelry and Accessories, Painted Wall Art, Screen Printed Accessories, No-Sew Fleece Quilt

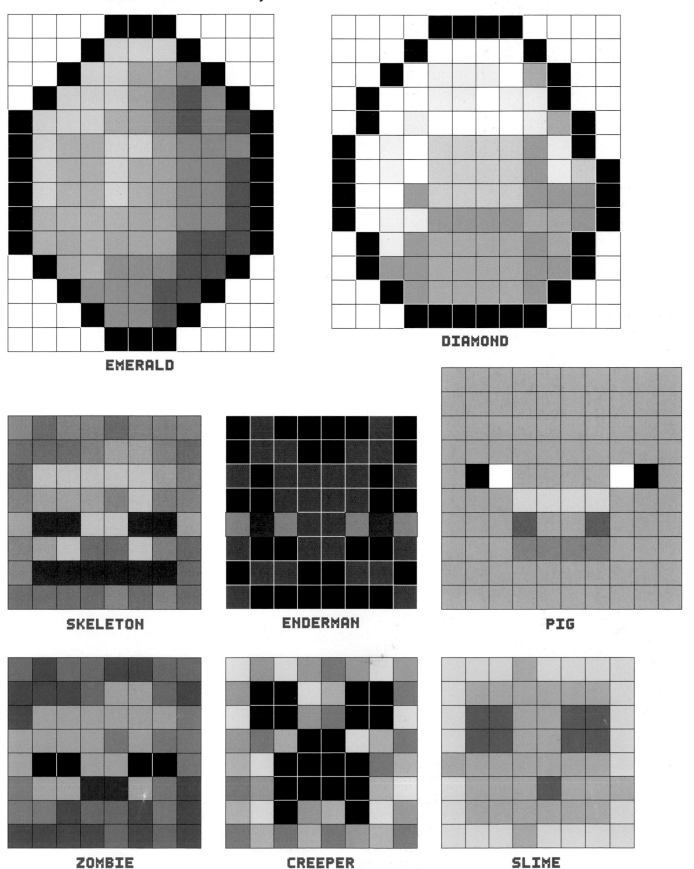

EMERALD

DIAMOND

SKELETON

ENDERMAN

PIG

ZOMBIE

CREEPER

SLIME

Pixel Plant

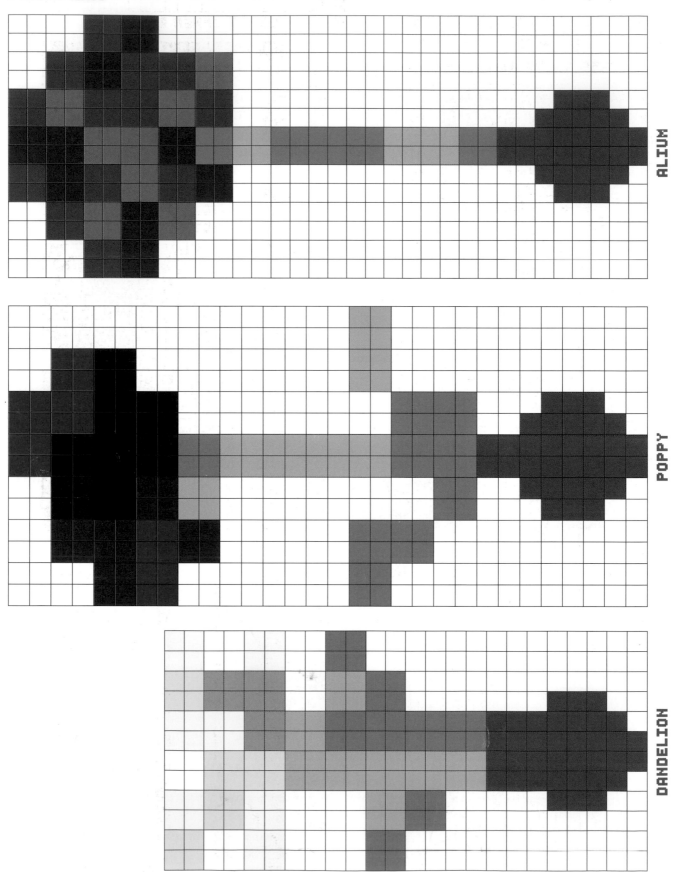

ALIUM

POPPY

DANDELION

Perler Bead Coin Box

GRASS INNER RIDGE X4

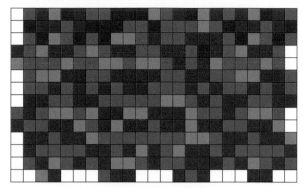

GRASS BOTTOM SIDE X4

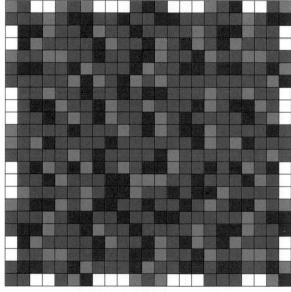

GRASS BOTTOM X1

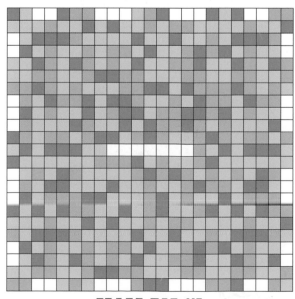

GRASS TOP X1

LATCH X1

CHEST INNER RIDGE X4

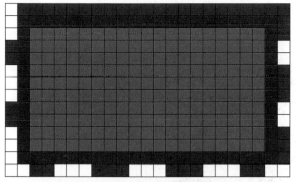

CHEST BOTTOM SIDE X4

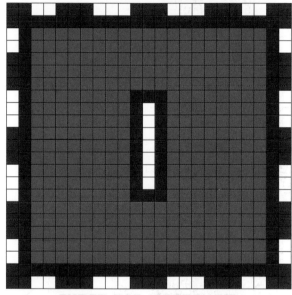

CHEST TOP/BOTTOM X2

*for bottom, fill coin slot with more light brown

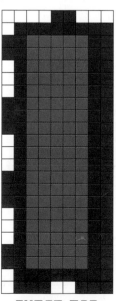

CHEST TOP SIDE X4

GRASS TOP SIDE X4

Duct Tape Wallet, End-of-the-Roll Box, Screen Printed Accessories, Felt Plush Cube, Crocheted Creeper

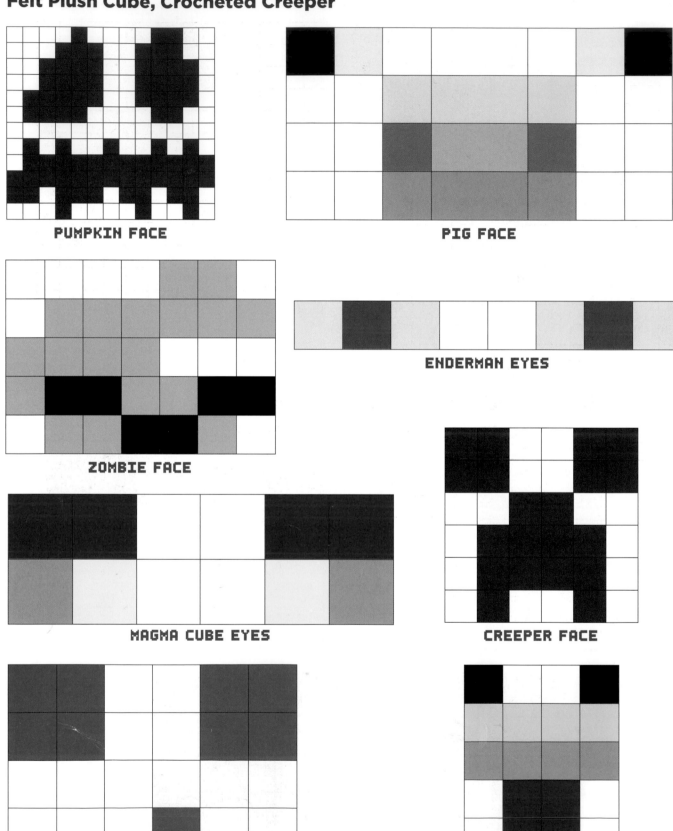

PUMPKIN FACE

PIG FACE

ZOMBIE FACE

ENDERMAN EYES

MAGMA CUBE EYES

CREEPER FACE

SLIME FACE

CHICKEN FACE

Foam Tools

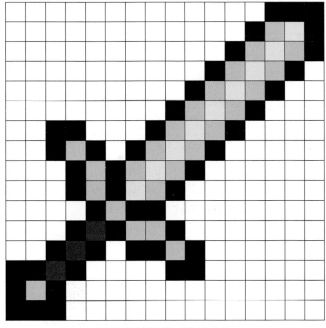

DIAMOND SWORD

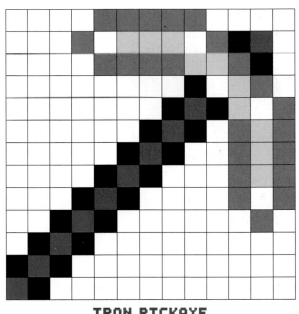

IRON PICKAXE

Cardboard Costume Head, Painted Wall Art

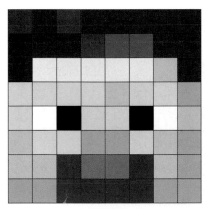

FRONT

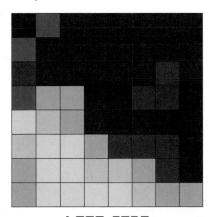

LEFT SIDE

BACK

RIGHT SIDE

TOP

Flashlight Torch

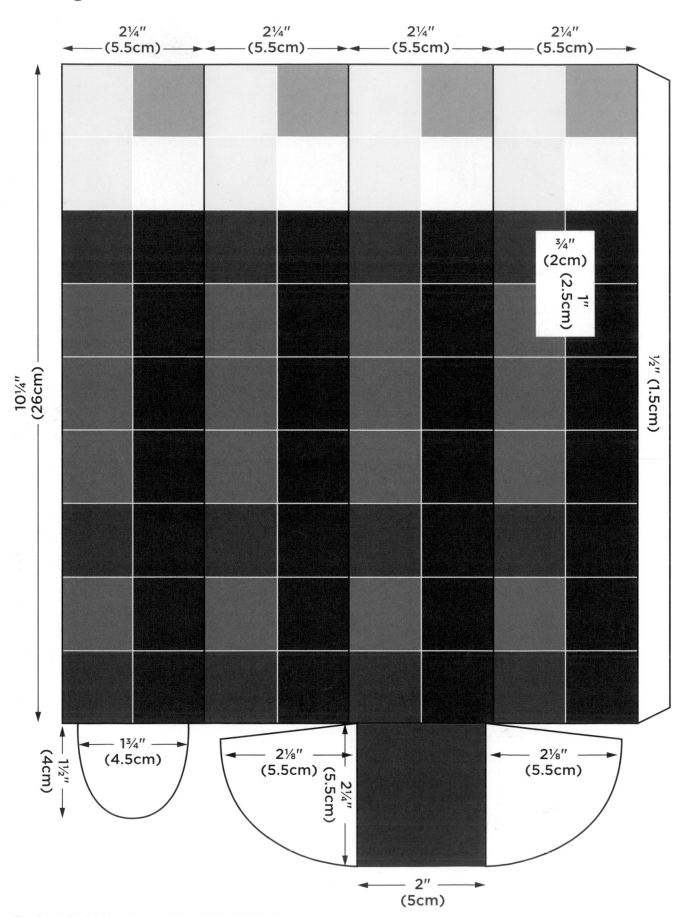

2¼″ (5.5cm) 2¼″ (5.5cm) 2¼″ (5.5cm) 2¼″ (5.5cm)

¾″ (2cm) 1″ (2.5cm)

½″ (1.5cm)

10¼″ (26cm)

1¾″ (4.5cm) 1½″ (4cm) 2⅛″ (5.5cm) 2¼″ (5.5cm) 2⅛″ (5.5cm)

2″ (5cm)

Ore Light

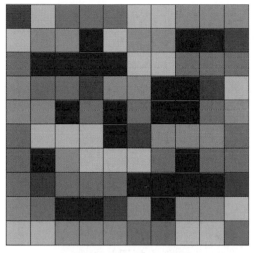

REDSTONE ORE

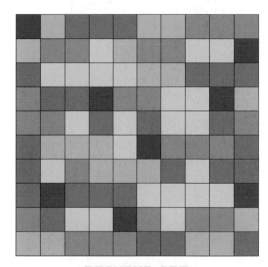

DIAMOND ORE

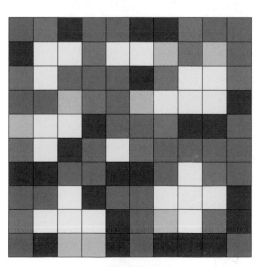

GLOWSTONE

Building Blocks

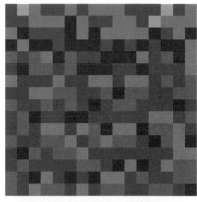

GRASS BLOCK SIDE X1

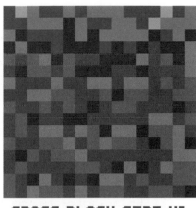

GRASS BLOCK SIDE X1

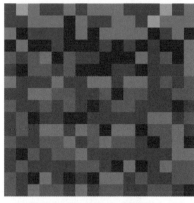

GRASS BLOCK SIDE X1

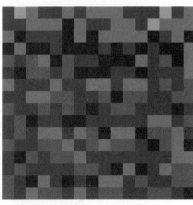

GRASS BLOCK SIDE X1

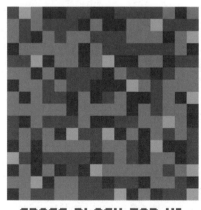

GRASS BLOCK TOP X1

GRASS BLOCK BOTTOM X1

Building Blocks

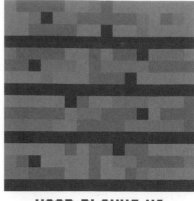

WOOD PLANKS X6

BRICK X6

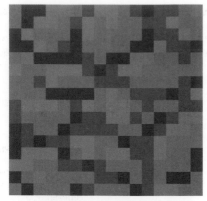

COBBLESTONE X6

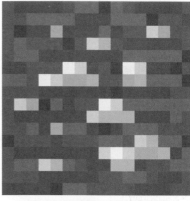

DIAMOND ORE X6

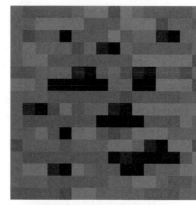

REDSTONE ORE X6

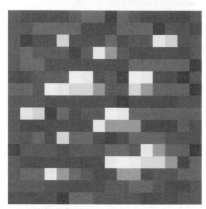

GOLD ORE X6

TNT BLOCK SIDE X2

TNT BLOCK SIDE X2

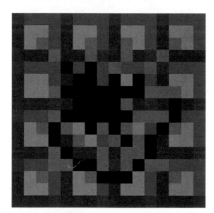

TNT BLOCK TOP/BOTTOM X2

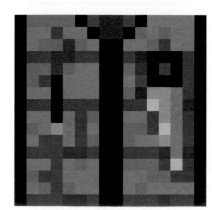

CRAFTING TABLE SIDE X2

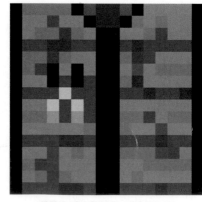

CRAFTING TABLE SIDE X2

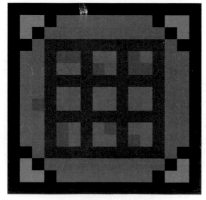

CRAFTING TABLE TOP/BOTTOM X2

INDEX

Note: Page numbers in *italics* indicate projects and patterns.

- -

GALLERY CONTRIBUTORS

Pages 6–7:
Angie Lee, *pinkapronconfections.com*
Halle Harrington, *hallecake.net*
Loren Ebert, *thebakingsheet.blogspot.com*
Caroline "CazGirl" Richardson, *cazgirl.tumblr.com*
Debbie Walsh, *maplespice.com*
Mellisa Swigart & Jeremy Swigart II, *momluck.com*
Janine Eshelbrenner, *sugarkissed.net*

Pages 8–9:
Jenn Desrochers of Momma D and Da Boyz, *MommaDandDaBoyz.net*
Margarette Sia, *MargaretteSia.com*

Carol Colón, Partylicious, *partyliciouseventspr.blogspot.com*
Melissa Smith, *parties4ever.blogspot.com*
Rin Smith, *etsy.com/shop/Rinyrinri*

Pages 10–11:
Gina House, *ginahouse.net*
Laboratory 424, *lab424.com*
Laura Hutchison (PlayDrMom), *blog.playdrhutch.com*
Ruth Seibt, *etsy.com/shop/CastleRainCreations*
Gem Battle, *facebook.com/inthewitchwood*

Pages 12–13:
Brenda Ponnay, *alphamom.com*

Tina Stapleford, *CraftingNerdy.com*
Tina Vuotto (FrostBittenFox), *etsy.com/shop/Frostbittenfox*
L. Topp, *etsy.com/shop/elletoppdesignworks*
ceemdee, *ceemdee.deviantart.com*
Tyler Parkerson, *jennventures.com*
Denise Bertacchi, *stlMotherhood.com*

Pages 14–15:
William C. Jones, *williamcjones48.deviantart.com*
Vincent Ho, *holygrassblock.com*
Anna Allen (touken2), *touken2.deviantart.com*
Tina Alfredsen, *griffsnuff.deviantart.com*
Declan Bachwirtz, *minecraftphotography.deviantart.com*

PEG COUCH
Acquisition editor

KATIE WEEBER
Copy editor

COLLEEN DORSEY
Editor

JASON DELLER
Cover & layout designer

SCOTT KRINER
Project photographer

MATTHEW MCCLURE
Step-by-step photographer

ISBN 978-1-57421-966-1

Minecraft® is a registered trademark of Notch Development AB. Neither Fox Chapel Publishing nor the contributors to *Craft Projects for Minecraft® and Pixel Art Fans* are associated with, nor is this book sponsored by, Notch Development AB.

The following photos on pages 3–5 have been used under Creative Commons licenses. Photos #2 (by See Inside), #5 (by CananZembil), #8 (by Crystal), #23 (by Paolo Trabattoni), and #29 (by essie) have been used under the Creative Commons Attribution 2.0 Generic (CC BY 2.0) license. Photos #10 (by Nick Gray), #20 (by donielle g), and #25 (by Jim Trottier) have been used under the Creative Commons Attribution-ShareAlike 2.0 Generic (CC BY-SA 2.0) license. Photos #1 (by Acdx), #6 (by Zde), #17 (by MOs810), #18 (by MOs810), and #27 (by Axel Pixel) have been used under the Creative Commons Attribution-ShareAlike 3.0 Unported (CC BY-SA 3.0) license. To learn more, visit *http://creativecommons.org/licenses.*

The following photos on pages 3–5 were provided by *Fotolia.com*: #3, #52065255 Crossword © Vlad Ivantcov; #9, #33115508 Salon moderne © Uolir; #15, #50590184 Patchwork quilt © perlphoto; #19, #56975799 Uncinetto © silviapezzola.

Additional credits for photos on pages 3–5: #24 courtesy Peter Bennetts, *www.peterbennetts.com*; #4, #7, #12, #13, #14, #16, #21, #22, #26, #28 courtesy *istockphoto.com*; #11 courtesy Alex Pu, "Pixel Painter", *http://demonstrations.wolfram.com/PixelPainter*, Wolfram Demonstrations Project, Published March 21, 2014.

© 2014 by Choly Knight and New Design Originals Corporation, *www.d-originals.com*, an imprint of Fox Chapel Publishing, 800-457-9112, 1970 Broad Street, East Petersburg, PA 17520.

Printed in the United States of America
First printing